Discipline:

Who Needs It?

Susan Cauley and Barry McCarty

Convention Press
Nashville, Tennessee

ISBN 0-7673-2000-X

Dewey Decimal Classification Number: 649
Subject Heading: DISCIPLINE OF CHILDREN//CHILDREN'S CHOIRS

Printed in the United States of America

Church Music Department
The Sunday School Board of the Southern Baptist Convention
127 Ninth Avenue, North
Nashville, Tennessee 37234

Editorial Staff
Clinton E. Flowers
Editor
Anne L. Trudel
Assistant Editor
Bill F. Leach
Senior Manager
Preschool/Children's Materials
Development Section

Design Staff
Mike Battenberg
Artist-Designer
Peggy McAdams
Format Writer

Contents

Introduction

by SUSAN CAULEY

Discipline: who needs it? is an important question. Chances are you already know the answer.

With the passage of time, the word *discipline* has received some added connotations ("to punish" or "to bring under control"). However, *discipline* originally comes from the Latin word *disciplina*, which means "teaching" or "learning." Therefore, in its best sense, **to discipline is to train or develop by teaching.**

The process of being disciplined begins at birth. A newborn quickly learns whether her cries of hunger will evoke a response from a caretaker. The process continues through every age and stage of life. Even senior adults are happiest and most productive when they are being disciplined—taught or instructed. Who needs discipline? We all do!

Music, that unique art which unites mind and spirit to express emotion, requires remarkable discipline in all its facets. Couple that with the group dynamic of a choir setting, add the unrelenting exuberance of children, and you have a situation which calls for discipline in massive doses!

Our scriptural directive for discipline is clear: "Teach and instruct one another with all wisdom. Sing psalms, hymns, and sacred songs; sing to God with thanksgiving in your hearts" (Colossians 3:16, GNB).[1] Who needs discipline in preschool and children's choirs? Both the children *and* their adult leaders need it—preferably in continual, generous measure.

Let's focus on you, the preschool or children's choir leader. The fact that you are reading this book is a positive indication that you are concerned about discipline in your choir. Perhaps you, like many teachers today, are frustrated with children's lack of discipline.

Before we discuss the children's behavior, however, consider some ways that you, the leader, should be disciplined. Prepare a mental checklist and rate yourself with regard to the following:

☐ **Knowing the children.** Preschool and children's choir leaders should know about children *developmentally.* Learn what the experts say about the age group with which you work. What are this age's characteristic behavioral and growth patterns?

Choir leaders should also know the children in their choir *individually.* Visit in each child's home. Have one-on-one conversations with children about important matters in their lives. Plan appropriate social gatherings which allow you to relate to the boys and girls in different, less formal settings.

☐ **Seeking knowledge.** Attend music leadership conferences and workshops. Read books and periodicals related to preschool and children's choirs. Talk to and observe fine teachers and other choir leaders. Be open to new and different ways of doing choir. Become a sponge—soak up all the knowledge you can about choir leadership.

☐ **Planning ahead.** Develop the discipline of planning with your choir teaching team. In the summer, plan for the entire year. Each month, plan the upcoming unit. Plan well in advance for special programs and events.

☐ **Preparing for each rehearsal.** Be especially disciplined in your preparation for that brief, precious block of time you spend with the children each week. Consider carefully how you will sequence and pace the rehearsal or large-group and small-group activities. Know your music down to the smallest detail. Have "emergency tactics" on hand for dealing with unexpected snags. Plan for variety and fun!

☐ **Preparing the environment.** Room arrangement and visuals play a crucial role in choir management. Arrange the children's chairs in a circle, semicircles, or rows according to your desired outcome. Visual aids and room decorations should be eye-catching but not so cluttered as to distract. Make sure in advance that all audiovisual equipment is in place and working properly.

□ **Maintaining a prayerful attitude.** If, as the hymn writer put it, prayer is "the soul's sincere desire, unuttered or expressed,"[2] then discipline calls us to be constantly in the prayer mode. In thought as well as in deed, our sincere desire must be for the physical, emotional, social, spiritual, and musical development of each child and his or her family. Pray for your coleaders in the music ministry. Pray for understanding, perspective, and a *positive spirit.* Viewing God as a partner in the teaching process brings encouragement and calm to the awesome task of leading preschool and children's choirs.

How did you rate yourself in each of these areas? If you are highly disciplined and well-prepared, a surprising fringe benefit is that your children will often respond with more cooperative behavior.

Many adults sing the blues about children's rudeness or lack of control. "How can I get them to change?" they desperately ask. But this is the wrong question. Ultimately, who is the only person you have the power and permission to change? You guessed it—yourself. Instead, ask yourself the question "How can *I* change the way I teach and relate to these children?" That will yield far more valuable results.

Okay, suppose you made a strong showing in each of the above aspects of self-discipline. Still, you have recurring behavioral problems in choir rehearsal. So do I! I write about this subject not as an expert, but as a survivor. The truth is that, although children pass through the same stages of development they always have, their environment is increasingly complex. Teaching children today *is* more difficult than it was when I began working with children's choirs 20 years ago. The central portion of this book (the scenarios on pages 15-47) is intended to offer the disciplined leader several options for dealing with some typical choir behavioral problems. Read it with your own choir children in mind, and remember—we *all* need discipline!

---

[1]This quotation is from the *Good News Bible*, the Bible in Today's English Version. Old Testament: Copyright © American Bible Society 1976; New Testament: Copyright © American Bible Society 1966, 1971, 1976. Used by permission.
[2]From the hymn "Prayer Is the Soul's Sincere Desire." Words by James Montgomery, 1818.

Music and Children

by BARRY McCARTY

We carry music—the notes, words, and sounds—within us from childhood. To a child, music is visual, physical, emotional, social, and spiritual.

The meaning and power of a song or phrase are highly personal. As a child, I often sang songs at the top of my lungs as I swung in my backyard. If I was thinking about church, I sometimes sang "Onward Christian Soldiers." I expressed strong thoughts and feelings by singing hymns wherever I was and whatever I was doing.

While our world view and personal experiences change and deepen us, the simple songs and ideas of our childhood give us emotional, physical, and spiritual comfort and release throughout our lives. In other words, what we learn as children stays with us throughout our lives.

As a choir director or leader, you have the opportunity to add to the development of young hearts and minds by blending music with the great themes and energy of the Old and New Testaments. Music and the practice of making music will help a whole new generation of young believers grow both musically and spiritually. Music helps us relax and cooperate as we blend voices, emotions, and personalities. Choir gives us a place to regularly practice a sense of community, cooperation, and the sharing of gifts, abilities, and perceptions.

As our Creator, God put into our original makeup a love of singing and expressing ourselves. As a choir leader, you have many opportunities to learn how to harness great stores of physical, emotional, mental, and spiritual energy and awareness. Teaching children in choir requires patience, inspiration, discipline, acceptance, leadership, kindness, and communication.

Young children are open to all kinds of music. They listen with interest, joy, and excitement to new words, new and old sounds, and ideas. Children's hearts and minds are open to the beauty, energy, and soon-familiar words and tunes that we present to them.

While a child is learning to listen to music— to make friends with the words and music—he responds to music at many different levels: his physical, emotional, and mental states are absorbing and reacting to how music sounds and feels. Children also watch each other to see how the music affects their friends and peers. A social and personal need for the experience of music is always a part of children's work and play.

A child explores and evaluates the personalities of other children and his teacher, and how they relate to each other. If you like children and music and you want the choir experience to be fun, exciting, and varied, children will notice and respond to your friendliness and to your energy. Children need to know that you like them and are interested in what they are doing. They need to know that you like music, and that you know what you are doing. While you need to be prepared each week (to have a lesson plan), you also need to meet children where they are and know their limits of attention, energy, and interest. Remember that you get these children in the middle of a long and structured school week and in a life-style that is typically quite demanding and rushed.

As a father and as a child and family therapist, I have learned the importance of knowing the distinct developmental stages and milestones that children go through from infancy through adolescence. Books like Fitzhugh Dodson's *How to Parent*[1] and *How to Father*[2] can give teachers and parents good information and valuable insight into children's needs, issues, and abilities at every stage of development.

Knowing what is normal and typical behavior for a particular age child is helpful, even if you have children of many different ages in your choir. Remember that children are constantly interacting with life, school, peers, teachers, and family and that they relate to different styles of authority and discipline.

[1]Fitzhugh Dodson, *How to Parent* (New York: NAL-Dutton, 1971).
[2]Fitzhugh Dodson, *How to Father* (New York: NAL-Dutton, 1975).

Note: a more recent book by Dodson, *How to Discipline with Love.* was published by NAL-Dutton in 1987.

Music and Children

Making Discipline Work

by SUSAN CAULEY

When I talk with other children's choir leaders about choir management, the problems they describe have a decidedly familiar ring. Their sixth-grade girls remind me of the ones who were in my Older Children's Choir last year. I know some seven-year-olds who behave much like the ones they describe. And our church's Preschool Choir director has management problems that match up with theirs almost to the detail!

Each child is unique, as God intended; yet all follow the same general developmental sequence and many are exposed to similar stresses in today's complex environment. So at least *some* behavior problems are common to choirs of many shapes, sizes, and locations. The following scenarios describe "typical" choir management problems. If you haven't come across them in your own choir, sit tight for a year or two; your turn will probably come sooner than you'd prefer!

Naturally, describing these scenarios is easier than encountering them live in the choir room. Understand that this book's suggestions should not be seen as "pat" answers to unusual or complex problems. There is no way to give on these pages a "quick fix" for managing your choir; multiple factors make each situation unique. With this in mind, I offer possible practical alternatives—things to do "behind the scenes"—that have worked for me and for other choir leaders. Barry responds to the scenarios with observations from his perspective as a child and family therapist. Whenever possible, I include a guideline—an important principle that applies to many situations and is worth remembering. The guidelines are shaded in grey.

Learn everything possible about your children's needs, both individual and collective. Then, keeping the guidelines in mind, create practical solutions which nurture each child's self-esteem and encourage optimal learning for the entire group.

Scenario 1

When Everyone
Is Talking

At tonight's rehearsal, everyone seems to have been bitten by the same bug. The children are cooperative—as long as they are singing or actively involved in something. But the moment you stop to give directions or explanations, they instantly start talking. And it isn't just one or two "troublemakers," either; it's almost everybody. No one is doing anything terribly rude or obnoxious; they're just talking! Reclaiming their attention takes so much time that you are unable to get through half of your planned activities.

Things to Do

1. **Take emergency measures.** Say, loudly and firmly (but with some degree of Christian love), "FREEZE!" Then, while the children are still in shock, whisper: "This is a time to listen for instructions. Please turn in your *Music Makers* magazine to . . ."

Or try this. In a strong voice, command: "Look at the ceiling. Look at the light switch. Look at the door frame. Look at me." Now

speak softly: "Please put your magazine under your chair, take out your hymnal, and turn to Hymn Number 75."

2. **Be flexible.** Children in my choirs have taught me a new beatitude: "Blessed are the flexible, for they shall not get bent out of shape." Before you get too angry about children talking in choir, consider certain adult choir rehearsals where the same phenomenon occurs!

Many years passed before I figured out that if the accompanist and I launch into a hymn or song, the children will stop talking and join us. Doing this is much quicker than waiting to get their attention. Of course, the skills we must teach in choir include watching the director, listening for instructions, breathing with the preparatory beat, and so forth. At times, however, the best option is to move on and let the children catch up with you.

Try *not* to stop and lecture the children.

> **Guideline:** The fewer times you stop the flow of things and confront the children negatively, the better.

Occasionally confronting the children negatively is necessary, but I go to great lengths to avoid it. Why? Simply because confrontations are interruptive, and they often leave a bad taste in everyone's mouth. Then choir is not as much fun.

3. **Keep things moving.** Are you, the director, talking too much? On an evening when all the children are talking, you probably should keep words to a minimum. Save lengthy, inspiring discourses for a night when everyone is more attentive.

Have your agenda well in mind, so that as one song or activity ends, you can move immediately into the next. For example, at the end of a song or anthem, while your hands are still in the cut-off position and the children have not yet had a chance to breathe, say, "Now look at that poster and clap the beats from left to right." This skill takes practice and comes more naturally for some directors than for others, but it can dramatically improve the flow of activity in large group.

4. **Move on to something else.** Know your rehearsal plans well. If the children are talking and seem to have lost interest in what is happening, move to the next step in your rehearsal plans. Or insert an activity into your rehearsal plans that is a sure attention getter—something you know the children will enjoy.

5. **Give children a time to talk.** Consider having a two-minute break in the middle of large group when the children can talk to their hearts' content. Agree in advance on a signal to end the talking break, and proceed with the rehearsal.

The signal to stop talking could be a chord played on the piano or a rhythm pattern played on a classroom instrument of your choice. A timer with an alarm is also a good possibility.

Comments from a Child Therapist

Talking is a way for children of all ages to relax and to let out emotions and ideas that have been bottled up through a busy day. Choir leaders should not take children's incessant talking too personally.

Giving the children structured time (from three to five minutes) to talk is a good idea. When you give children structured time to talk, you take control by directing an activity that they want to do anyway! If something major has happened that day at school or in the nation or world (such as a war, earthquake, or end of a war), take time to talk together about the event and explore the children's feelings about it before starting a planned activity. A group prayer for the people affected may be powerful and healing to everyone.

Choir and church are social as well as religious and spiritual activities. As children get older (especially eight-year-olds, ten-year-olds, and twelve-year-olds), their peer relationships become their main mirrors for knowing how they are doing and whether they are "cool."

Lecturing or stopping to correct or criticize a preadolescent who talks too much will not help your relationship with that child. In fact, it may cause the child to resent your authority and resist your plans—something that neither you nor the group needs.

Keep in mind that preadolescents are very sensitive to personal criticism, especially in public or in front of their peers. If you need to clear the air with them, do it individually and in private. Include positive comments, and you may be able to build a friendship rather than an unforgiving, adversarial relationship.

Leaders should model what they want. This helps children of all ages know what is expected of them.

The advice to keep things moving during rehearsal is good. Leaders' expectations and agenda must fit the abilities and interests of the children they work with. Leaders need to be flexible, friendly, and have clear goals and plans in order to help their choir feel like they are accomplishing something concrete, interesting, and valuable.

Scenario 2

Lethargy in Large Group

It is large-group time. A carefully worked-out rehearsal plan lies on the music stand, and you launch into it with fervor. But just three minutes later, the knowledge dawns that your choir is present in body but not in spirit. The children's posture is sloppy; their eyes are wandering. In the middle of a fun song, someone asks what time it is. You would be hard-pressed to discover the children exerting an ounce of energy. Your singers are lethargic, and because proper singing requires so much energy, you look for ways to energize them.

Things to Do

1. **Acknowledge that the children may really be tired; give them permission to admit it.** If your rehearsal occurs before or after the evening meal on Wednesday, think about the amount of work and/or play that has already filled each child's day. "But," you may respond, "I just saw those same children running through the halls. They *can't* be tired!" They may not look tired, but you need to

remember that many children increase their activity level as they become fatigued. Simply sitting down in the choir room may be all it takes for the reality of exhaustion to set in.

If space permits, take an FOYB (Flat On Your Back) break. In the middle of large-group time, or whenever lethargy seems to have taken charge, say: "FOYB! You have 30 seconds to silently find a spot where you can lie flat on your back without touching anyone or anything." Encourage the children to relax, breathe deeply, and listen to soothing instrumental music (a recording or your accompanist) for three minutes. Then, as an adult leader touches them, they may return quietly to their seats.

If floor space is not available, a similar rest break may be taken by having the children assume "movie position" (the posture often assumed when watching movies—sliding the buttocks forward on the chair and resting the neck on the chair's back).

Following this brief, concerted rest break, proceed with your original rehearsal plans.

2. Heighten the children's level of concern by simulating a performance environment in the rehearsal. If just a fraction of the nervous excitement that energizes a performance can be invoked in the choir room, lethargy will become a thing of the past.

20

An audience is the key ingredient, and providing one is easier than you might think. Before having the children sing through a song or anthem, tell them that their adult leaders will be looking for energy they can see, hear, and feel. When the choir has finished, ask the leaders to report.

Learn to rely on that trusty friend, the tape recorder. Keep a recorder handy with a blank tape so that at any time during rehearsal, you can say, "Let's sing that again and see if this machine picks up those crisp final consonants." It is incredible how children shape up when they are confronted with the unbiased ear of the tape recorder. Be sure to give them something specific to listen for as you play the recording back.

Inviting guests to the choir rehearsal provides an excellent low-stress performance opportunity. Children grow weary of interacting with the same adults in choir week after week. Ask the minister of music, the organist, or a couple of parents to come to rehearsal and listen to an anthem. Have the guest or guests watch for eyes on the director, perfect posture, or whatever singing skill you are currently stressing. If the guest happens to be a singer or a church musician, he or she might talk with the children about a prearranged topic which enriches the children's choir experiences. Having a different adult visit rehearsal every month or so will go a long way toward reducing lethargy.

3. **Try some body energizers.** If the children's lethargy appears to be a result of boredom or laziness, try some body energizers for about 30 seconds to bring them back physically and mentally. Here are some quick energizers:

• Have the children stand and bend forward at the waist, dangling their arms and heads. While they are bent over, have them shake their arms vigorously.

• Ask the children to straighten to an upright standing position. Have them rotate their heads slowly from left to right eight times.

• Have them stand on their tiptoes and reach for the ceiling eight times.

• Ask the children to put their hands on their waists, with elbows pointing out to the sides. Have them roll their shoulders to the back eight times, then to the front eight times.

These are only a few body energizers. You can become adept at creating your own.

Comments from a Child Therapist

When they are especially fatigued, give children a few minutes to talk about their day. Ask them to share the best thing that happened, then the worst thing. You can make this a verbal, around-the-group exercise or an individual exercise that is written and not shared. Both are good ways to get children to let go of the day and focus on new activities.

Some lethargy may be due to negative things that happened at school or on the way to church. For example, a child may be deeply worried and tense about an upcoming test or a school project that is due the next day. Get children to verbalize their fears and anxieties. Then encourage them to talk about summer plans, vacations, or what they want to do when they are grown. This will help your group of children join the present moment and activity and will better prepare them to be influenced by music.

Susan's suggestion for a FOYB break with soft background music is wonderful. You can extend this into a visualization exercise by telling the children to think of something they enjoy doing and to imagine themselves doing it. To help them visualize, tell them to think about what they see, hear, and feel as they are doing their enjoyable activity.

Participating in such an exercise as the one described above can both calm and energize the children. When they have permission to soar with their minds and take leave of their worries and fears for a few minutes on a regular basis, they can then come back to the present feeling more relaxed and refreshed.

It is a great idea to invite guests to a rehearsal both to critique and to encourage children who may be tired of the routine and same choir group. You could also have a guest storyteller take three to five minutes to tell about an experience he or she had in choir, school, or life. Stories and storytellers give children a fresh perspective and a chance to broaden their range of life experiences.

Think of creative ways to encourage and enrich your choir children's hearts and minds. Doing this regularly keeps life and music adventuresome, interesting, and unpredictable!

Scenario 3

Climbing the Walls from the Very Start

All is ready. A choir leader is waiting with activities in hand for early arrivers. Small-group areas have been meticulously prepared. The appearance of the room says, "Come and learn; this will be fun!"

Then the children begin to enter. When the first three children bound into the room scuffling and shouting, you suspect that today's rehearsal will be one of "those" rehearsals.

Five wild and wooly minutes later, your suspicions are confirmed. The noise level mounts steadily. Children run from one activity to the next. Getting them settled and "on task" seems an impossibility.

Things to Do

1. **Take emergency measures.** Don't assume that you must endure inappropriate behavior to stick with your original plans. Do something quickly!

Obviously, very little learning is taking place in the above scenario. The other choir leaders will probably appreciate your taking im-

mediate action to regain order.

If your room arrangement allows, forget small groups and switch gears to something everyone can do together. Echoing body rhythms (example: clapping) or just singing a familiar song are good choices for redirecting the energy and capturing the attention of a rambunctious group. Keep these and other emergency measures in your hip pocket. Be ready to abandon your previous plans and implement these emergency measures when the situation requires a drastic change.

2. **Establish clear guidelines.** If the scenario depicted in this chapter is not unusual for your group, you need to make the children aware of exactly what they can and cannot do in choir. Clearly spell out incentives for following the guidelines, as well as consequences for breaking them. This type of assertive discipline plan may be necessary to reverse tough problems and encourage optimum learning. Be thoughtful, fair, and positive as you formulate and administer

your plan.

Display your choir rules in a prominent spot, and consistently reinforce them. Some directors let the boys and girls make their own rules, thereby giving them ownership in the plan for guiding behavior. If you take this approach, expect the children to make lots of rules and to have some trouble wording them positively.

You may discover that fewer rules will be easier to enforce. Through the years I have honed and whittled my list of choir rules down to two:

1. Sing with energy.
2. Treat others with respect.

Rarely am I confronted with a behavior problem which is not covered by one of these two rules.

Guideline: As any behaviorist will tell you, positive reinforcement is more effective than negative reinforcement, and it certainly makes for a more pleasant atmosphere in the choir room. Always be on the lookout to "catch" children who are behaving appropriately; be specific as you encourage that behavior.

"Jamie, you kept your eyes on me throughout that song. That made it possible for us to sing those final consonants exactly together. Thank you!" or "Jake, you were listening carefully to directions. That helped you to play the Autoharp correctly." Both these statements are more specific and helpful than simply saying "Good job!" or "That was great!"

If a more concrete incentive seems necessary, give the children ways to earn privileges or small treats by behaving appropriately in choir. Remember that younger children need more immediate rewards, while older children may be able to earn their rewards over a longer period of time. Select an incentive which will be appealing to the children and approved by their parents. (For example, if your choir rehearses before dinner, or if some parents disapprove, awarding candy or sweet treats would be unwise.)

Then formulate a plan which can be implemented with as little maintenance as possible. Here are two plans, one for younger children and one for older, that have worked for me.

This plan was devised for a group of first, second, and third graders who were behaving much like the children described in Scenario 3. The rules for choir behavior, as well as a chart displaying each child's name followed by three stickers, were posted before the group.

An adult leader (not the director) was in charge of monitoring the group's behavior. Whenever someone broke a rule, the leader removed one of that child's stickers from the chart. At the end of choir, each child received the same number of small treats (candy or sugarless gum) as there were stickers left by his or her name.

The following plan was used with fourth, fifth, and sixth graders. Each week before large group, a horizontal line was drawn on the chalkboard beneath the choir rules. Whenever one or more rules were being broken, the director said nothing, but simply erased a bit of the line. If even a smidgen of the line was left at the end of the rehearsal, the group received a point for the day, recorded at another place on the chalkboard. The choir earned a pizza party by accumulating eight points.

> **Guideline:** Note that in both these plans, the emphasis is on the positive (earning treats or privileges for appropriate behavior), rather than on the negative. In neither case does the flow of teaching have to be interrupted to acknowledge inappropriate behavior.

If you feel an assertive discipline plan is necessary in your own choir, formulate a plan that best suits your needs. No plan will continue to be effective over a long period of time, so be prepared to change the plan after a few weeks or months.

Be especially careful when establishing a reward system with preschoolers. Often a smile, touch, or word of encouragement is sufficient to motivate a preschooler; he will be confused by an involved system of points and incentives.

Comments from a Child Therapist

Some groups of children and their chemistry together require much adult teamwork in setting boundaries and enforcing discipline. Some children need much physical and emotional activity and exertion before they can settle down enough to listen and to let music comfort and nurture them.

If you have such a group of children who are especially fired-up and collectively noisy and wild, remember that they are not necessarily acting this way to personally defeat your spirit and leadership abilities.

Keep a sense of humor, and commit yourself to setting reasonable, fair, and firm boundaries for the children. Providing time-out places for children to calm down and refocus will help.

Couple this with rewards for good behavior, like extra story time or game activities. Stickers and stamps are effective positive rewards for children up to age 7 or 8. A positive reinforcement method for older children (ages 9-11) is to appoint one child each week as superstar (helper) of the week. Let the child bring his or her baby picture the next week and lead some activity. Older children also enjoy candy treats. Another effective reward for this age group is to dismiss children at the end of choir in the order of good behavior displayed during choir. Giving the children physical chores to burn off their energy—such as helping you set up the room—may help those with high energy levels who need constant physical and emotional reassurance.

Become familiar with the developmental issues for the ages of children you teach. This will help you know what they are capable of giving and receiving.

You may need several high school student-assistants to help in your choir. Discipline needs to be consistent, fair, and uniform among all the teachers and assistants. There needs to be an ultimate authority in the room—one whom the other leaders will support and be loyal to and that the children will respect and yield to. That ultimate authority should be the director.

Keep in mind that loving each child is important, even when you really dislike a child's behavior or actions. Being positive is also important. I've heard and read that it takes five positive comments to overcome one negative one.

Most children eventually respond to a person who says what he or she means and means what he or she says. An effective, consistent system of discipline and unity among teachers are necessary to create an atmosphere of cooperation and group fun in learning to create music.

Scenario 4

The Short
Attention Span

Children with short attention spans can be found in any choir from preschool through older children. They are unable to concentrate for longer than a brief period of time.

While other children are still involved in a task, these children are toying with something in their pockets, poking at their neighbors, or staring out the window. When the choir sings a song or anthem, they "check out" after the first few words.

Whether the problem stems from simple immaturity or from a serious behavior disorder, these symptoms are often encountered in choir. You must deal with them creatively.

Things to Do

1. **Make sure these children are not distracting one another.** One remedy may be assigning seats in choir. Thoughtfully work out a seating arrangement which separates children who have trouble concentrating. Tape the children's names to the backs of chairs, or

designate the chairs with music folders which display the children's names. If you allow children to sit where they like, reserve the right to pleasantly and matter-of-factly separate those who seem to be distracting one another.

2. **Rethink the structure of the choir rehearsal.** If you want the children's optimum concentration during large group, try having small groups at the end. Evaluate your plans to determine whether you have a balance between active and inactive learning. Are you asking for longer periods of quiet, passive behavior than the children are able to deliver? A few changes in the order of things could make a decided difference.

Guideline: Always plan for variety in rehearsals. Aim for balance between:
- moving and sitting still
- singing and listening
- group and individual responses
- attention to the music in hand and attention toward the front of the room

The Short Attention Span

3. **Plan activities which gradually lengthen the children's attention while singing.** Ask a choir leader to watch and write down the number of children who concentrate and watch the director throughout one stanza of a song. When the leader reports that almost all the children have been successful (aiming for 100% may be unrealistic), try for two stanzas. Continue until most of the group are concentrating for the entire length of the song, hymn, or anthem.

Avoid writing on the chalkboard the names of those who are paying attention. This fosters competition between the children, and some react negatively if their names are omitted. Using numbers encourages a cooperative spirit among the group.

Guideline: Resist the temptation to rely heavily on competition as a motivator. Although many children are excited by a competitive activity, too often their focus is on the contest rather than the learning. Adults may not realize that some children find competition stressful and frustrating.

Comments from a Child Therapist

Children who have short attention spans or are easily distracted require much energy and attention from teachers to help them settle into a routine of listening and participating. Choir leaders also pay a high price for getting these children at the end of a long, structured school day.

Most children do not come to choir with the intention of driving their teachers and peers crazy. Separating easily distracted children is a great idea, and providing them with more encouragement and supervision may be necessary to keep the whole group on task.

If you have one or two choir children who are constantly inattentive (or even hostile to your suggestions or corrections), ask their parents if you can consult with their school teacher to see how he or she handles them over a full day. Consulting with the parents may be helpful so you can compare notes and plan a strategy for improving their child's participation and attention. Remember to be sensitive to the parents in this situation.

Attention-deficit problems may be due to hyperactivity; hearing problems; multiple stressors in the family; or worry, fear, and frustration in the child due to major changes or losses in the child's life. It is helpful for leaders to know and understand the child and to figure out what is causing the child's restlessness.

A child may be asking for help even through negative and provocative behavior. Consulting with other teachers and professionals may help you see if a pattern of restlessness and inattention permeates the child's life. Pediatricians can assess the physical symptoms and states of stress, and child therapists can evaluate the emotional, personal, and family dynamics that may contribute to the voluntary or involuntary inattention. Anything you can learn from professionals about a restless child can help you know how to better to harness the child's emotional and physical energy.

Scenario 5

The Child with a Special Need

A family that has recently joined your church has a child with cerebral palsy (or a hearing impairment, or attention deficit hyperactivity disorder, or some other handicap or disability). The child is the right age for your choir. You are apprehensive, but you want to include the child in choir if at all possible.

Things to Do

1. **Talk with the child's parents.** Are they interested in their child's participating in choir? Learn all you can from them about the nature of the child's abilities and disabilities. How does he respond to music in a group setting? How can you adapt the choir room and your teaching to help her?

2. **Talk with the child.** How does he view his special need? Does he enjoy music? Ask how he feels about coming to choir. You might introduce him to one or two other choir members ahead of time, so

there will be friendly, familiar faces in the choir room when he arrives.

3. **If necessary, enlist a competent, caring adult to care for and assist the child during choir.** For example, a child who lacks the use of her arms would benefit from having an adult hold her music and move her arms during body rhythm activities.

4. **With the parents' permission, talk briefly and matter-of-factly to the other children before the child comes to choir.** Help them know what to expect, and discuss ways they can help the new choir member feel welcome. When children understand the unique needs of a handicapped or disabled child, they usually go out of their way to be helpful to that child.

5. **Prepare your rehearsal room, instruments, and necessary visuals for the child with a handicap or disability.** First, be sure that the rehearsal room you select is accessible to the special-needs

The Child with a Special Need

child, particularly a child in a wheelchair. Place song charts, teaching pictures, and other visuals at a height and distance that allows all children (especially children who are visually handicapped or otherwise disabled) to see them comfortably.

Here are some things you can do to help children with visual handicaps: Use large letters when writing on the chalkboard. Label Autoharp chords, piano keys, step bells, and resonator bells with large, easily read letters. Give most of your instructions orally, since a child with a visual handicap may not be able to see whether you are pointing to a visual or to him.

A child with a physical disability may need assistance from a choir leader to play some musical instruments. The child may need to play the instrument in an unconventional manner. For a child in a wheelchair, leave space at the end of a row of chairs or provide another spot where the child can feel comfortable.

Seat a child with a hearing impairment near you or the source of sound, such as the record player. Be sure the child can see you well. When you teach a child who is hearing-impaired how to play an instrument, hold the instrument and demonstrate any verbal explanations. Speak distinctly. Look at the child as you speak. You will need to use a lot of visual aids such as pictures, physical gestures, and facial expressions.

6. **Prepare for children who are handicapped or disabled by reading books on the subject.**[1] Read books (and encourage other choir leaders to read books) about teaching children who are handicapped or disabled. Many excellent books on this topic are available at libraries and bookstores. Learn as much as you can about specific handicaps or disabilities of children in your choir.

7. **Consult a therapist to learn how to handle your special-needs child.** A therapist's advice will be a valuable aid to the total success of your choir rehearsals, as well as to the child having a beneficial, satisfying choir experience.

8. **Realize, and help the children realize, that they and their new friend are much more *alike* than *different*.**

Comments from a Child Therapist

If possible, talk to the special-needs child at length before introducing him or her to the other children. Find out how the child perceives his or her need or limitation. The child's attitude toward the disability or limitation matters a great deal, as does the parents' attitude toward the child's need.

Ask the child what he or she likes to do for fun. Invite him to tell you about his favorite subject at school and favorite hobbies or sports. Ask her what she misses about her previous church, school, or neighborhood. Ask the child what three wishes he would make if he could have anything come true.

Talk to the child's parents as well. What are the child's fears and worries? What are his or her gifts and talents? What are his or her strengths and weaknesses? With the parents' permission, talk to the child's schoolteachers, therapist, or special-needs coach.

Always remember that every child in your choir has particular gifts, strengths, and limitations. A child's way with words, humorous comments, or playful disposition can give energy to the group and to individual members. Each child needs to experience a feeling of success at performing, leading singing, drawing, or describing a feeling or idea that music tries to convey.

Since choir is primarily practice, let handicapped or disabled children participate from all the various vantage points, once they know what is expected of them. Don't ignore a child's special need, but see beyond it and help the child see how much the world needs his particular gifts, perceptions, and ideas.

---

[1] *Teaching Exceptional Persons* (Code # 5160-30), compiled by R. Wayne Bowen and Woody Parker (Convention Press, 1990), is available at Baptist Book Stores or by calling 1-800-458-2772.

Scenario 6

The Interrupter

Sometimes she tries, and sometimes she doesn't. But it seems that Martha absolutely cannot raise her hand and wait to be recognized before she speaks. If a question, comment, or answer enters her mind, she blurts it out fortissimo. (Note: Marthas abound in preschool and younger children's choirs; occasionally they appear in older children's choirs.)

Things to Do

1. **Ignore the behavior.** Someone has wisely said that a child should not be ignored. A child's behavior, on the other hand, may at times be wisely ignored.

   Guideline: Often it makes sense not to give any reinforcement, either positive or negative, to interruptive behavior.

2. **Give attention to someone who exhibits the desired behavior.** For example: "Brad, thank you for sitting quietly and raising your hand. Do you have a question?"

3. **Give the choir guidelines for a brief question-and-answer time during the rehearsal.** Try having one or more question-and-

answer times (from 30 seconds to 1 minute) during a rehearsal. Rehearsal time is valuable, so you need to be frugal with it. Setting a timer with a bell allows you to clearly terminate the question-and-answer time. A good time for specific questions related to the music is immediately after a song or anthem is rehearsed. Another good time for questions is at the end of the rehearsal. In fact, this may be your best time for questions and answers because the children will be eager to leave. A question-and-answer time may not be necessary every rehearsal. Use your discretion about how often to use this method.

4. **Invite the interrupter to stay after choir to ask questions.** This may discourage unnecessary questions. When he is asked to remain after choir, the interrupter may feel that his question or comment is not so important after all.

5. **Enlist your leaders' help.** At the beginning of the choir year, explain to the choir that children should direct questions that are unrelated to choir to one of the choir leaders. Leaders can take care of a child's personal needs without interrupting the rehearsal. Children often have questions about a forthcoming performance such as the date, time, and dress. These questions can be satisfactorily handled by an informed leader and not throw the rehearsal completely off track. Not having to deal with these types of questions can free

you to concentrate on what needs to be accomplished in the rehearsal.

Comments from a Child Therapist

Children, from before kindergarten on, know the rules that apply at home, in school, in church choir, and in worship services. When you deal with a child who has trouble controlling his or her impulses, the child's age matters a great deal, as does knowing what is going on in the child's life, both at home and at school.

In his book *The One-Minute Father,* Spencer Johnson suggests what I consider a wonderful way of dealing with unacceptable behavior. His technique, called the One-Minute Reprimand,[1] usually works with children from preschool age through early adolescence. Here is an adaptation of the One-Minute Reprimand for choir leaders. Remember that this technique should be done with a child in private, so you may need to ask the child to stay after choir.

1. **State how the child's actions made you feel.** For example, you might say: "What you did tonight in choir [specify the action] really made me angry (or frustrated or sad)!" Do not go on and on about the child's behavior; you can do this in as little as half a minute.

2. **Remain silent for several seconds.** This delay will make the child feel uncomfortable and resentful. The child will not like it, and he or she may not even like *you* at that moment. But the silence is necessary; you want to let the child feel what you felt. As you talk to the child, and during the silence, maintain eye contact with him or her.

3. **Let the child know that you are on his/her side and that even though you disliked the child's behavior, you still like him or her.** This part of the technique is crucial to its success. Say something like: "Your behavior tonight was not good. But *you* are good. The reason I got upset was because I know you're a good kid, and you can do better. And because I love you, I'll do anything I can to help you overcome this behavior!"

4. **When you finish the reprimand, it's over.** Do not mention it to the child again.

---

[1]Spencer Johnson, M.D., *The One-Minute Father* (New York: William Morrow and Company, Inc., 1983).

Scenario 7

"But I Didn't Get a Turn!"

Three instrumental parts accompany the song the choir is rehearsing, and time permits only a couple of run-throughs. Someone says, "But I didn't get a turn!"

The singing game calls for one child to sit in a chair while others stand around her in a circle and clap. At most, you have time to repeat the game four or five times. Someone whines, "But I didn't get a turn!"

The circumstances change, but the response is always the same. If children are being chosen for a task that everyone wants to do, without a doubt someone will cry, "But I didn't get a turn!"

Something to Do

Keep a set of "It's My Turn" cards handy. Write each choir member's name on an index card. Mix the cards and store them in an envelope attached to the wall or a nearby bulletin board. Whenever you must select a child to perform a task that everyone wants to do,

pull the first card from the envelope and announce the child's name. Then put that card at the back of the stack. Doing this eliminates wild hand-waving before the selection and hurt feelings afterward. Children of all ages seem to appreciate the fairness of this simple system.

Guideline: Fairness is extremely important to children. Although they may not always verbalize it, they will be grateful for every effort you make to be fair with them.

Comments from a Child Therapist

Children have an innate sense of justice and fairness. Even a toddler can tell if siblings have to live by the same rules. Children can tell instantly whether a child or adult likes them and is open to them, and whether they are being treated fairly. Children do not want to miss anything; their egos and wants are important, driving, and unavoidable!

Children at every age need assurance and praise because they struggle daily with many self-doubts and strong feelings of anger, fear, and sadness. They are often very hard on themselves. I once heard of a young child who refused to get out of the car and go into his kindergarten class because he didn't know how to read yet!

Sincere praise for a job well-done is important to everyone, especially children. Sincere praise, when it is deserved, sends a clear message to a child that he did a good job and that he can achieve the goals set before him. Praise gives a child a sense of confidence to try other more challenging tasks.

If you like and love each child you work with, each one will know at a deep level that you value who he or she is. The child will come to understand that you love her, even when you do not like some of the things she does.

The prerequisite for loving others, however, is loving ourselves. After all, Jesus said, "Thou shalt love thy neighbor as thyself" (Matthew 19:19). Only when we love ourselves sufficiently and kindly can we offer blessings and affirmations to the people who share our daily lives.

Over a period of time, try to call on each child in your choir, not just the extroverts who volunteer to do every activity and answer every question. Although a child may not get a turn when he thinks he should, he will appreciate the fact that he and his peers get an equal chance to participate in choir. The child will eagerly wait for his turn. When you are consistent in using a fair method for taking turns, the result will be fewer feelings of being left out or ignored.

Scenario 8

The Wandering Preschooler

Four-year-old Taylor participates enthusiastically in large group for a while. Suddenly, without warning, he simply stands up and walks away. He may head for an activity center or the window, or just wander aimlessly around, but he is definitely finished with what the group is doing.

Things to Do

1. **Enlist help from adult leaders.** One of your choir leaders can follow Taylor and either gently lead him back to the group or engage him in an individual activity which does not distract the other children. Some young children are simply not ready to stay in a group for more than a few minutes. If your choir includes several such wandering preschoolers, enlist extra leaders to help.

2. **Reevaluate the length and structure of your large-group period.**

- Are you expecting your preschoolers to spend too much time in

large group? Five or ten minutes can make a big difference to a very young child. A good rule of thumb for preschool music activity is: 7-10 minutes for early-arriver activities; 20-25 minutes for small-group activities; and 20 minutes for large-group activities. Remember that preschoolers will need about 5 minutes of transitional time between early-arriver activities and small-group activities, and between small-group activities and large group.

• Are you including enough movement activities in large group?

• Do you spend too much time on one song or activity before going on to the next? Be alert to nonverbal cues that indicate the children are ready to move on to something different. Here are some nonverbal clues children give: staring into space, looking around the room, squirming, taking a long breath, or shrugging shoulders.

Comments from a Child Therapist

For choirs of three-, four-, and five-year-olds, it is especially important for leaders to know the developmental tasks of each age—personally, physically, mentally, and socially. Encourage all of your leaders to read the sections on threes, fours, and fives from Fitzhugh Dodson's *How to Father*[1] or *How to Parent*.[2] Also, make these books

The Wandering Preschooler

available to all of your choir parents at the beginning of the choir year. If the parents are struggling to get along with a child at home, these books may offer them help. Pray for your choir parents and their children.

Most preschoolers have short attention spans for many activities. Much of a preschooler's play involves parallel play with his peers (playing near them) rather than direct interaction with them. Every preschooler is busy learning fine and gross motor skills while his or her social and verbal skills also are developing. Storytime can give children time to rest and relax while their minds and imaginations are busy working.

As you are probably aware, preschoolers are quite energetic. An interesting illustration of this fact is the experience of Jim Thorpe, a world-class Olympic athlete. Thorpe decided to mimic every physical move that a two-year-old made in a day's time. After two hours of copying the child's physical exertion of energy, Thorpe was exhausted and gave up. Likewise, guiding preschoolers in musical activities can often be trying and exhausting. Most energetic preschoolers require numerous creative activities to hold their attention.

Stressors in the family affect preschoolers dramatically and deeply. The birth of younger siblings, marital discord, and financial, social, or emotional stress in the family are changes in the life of a preschooler that add stress and worry. Many children may be having to adjust to their mothers going back to work. Others' families may have recently moved or struggled with illness or death.

Preschool choir members need hugs and lap time. These children need a lot of physical and emotional reassurance. They also respond well to playfulness. Once preschoolers feel comfortable with you, they can be quite affectionate.

Enjoy preschoolers' personalities and and give them plenty of different avenues to express their rich and bountiful levels of energy. Be there for them both emotionally and physically when they are angry or sad at the end of a demanding day.

---

[1]Fitzhugh Dodson, *How to Father* (New York: NAL-Dutton, 1975).
[2]Fitzhugh Dodson, *How to Parent* (New York: NAL-Dutton, 1971).

Scenario 9

The Bored Sixth Grader

Lauren has been in choir since she was four. Physically mature, she is now twelve going on sixteen and acts bored to tears. As she sits in your grades 4-6 choir, her body language says, "I'm too big for this stuff!" Each song or activity you suggest extracts a sigh from Lauren, as if it were all incredibly childish and far beneath her. Lauren has a couple of friends who have also contracted "sixth-grade-itis." The three of them are casting a bit of a pallor on the choir's spirit.

Things to Do

1. **Empathize.** Many sixth graders face a barrage of physical, emotional, and social changes. Like all fragile, precious beings, they must be handled with care.

Arrange to talk privately with your sixth graders. It will help them to hear you acknowledge and accept their feelings that choir is no longer as much fun as it once was. Emphasize that there is nothing wrong with those feelings; feelings belong to their owners, and as such they have no rightness or wrongness. The problem comes, however, when feelings are acted out in ways that distract others and prevent them from learning and having fun.

Explain specific ways that their behavior is affecting you and the group. As you show understanding for their feelings, they may begin to understand yours.

2. **Give them special privileges.** Coupling warm personal empathy with extra privileges goes a long way toward keeping sixth graders happy.

Assign some challenging early-arriver activities, solos, or instrumental parts to your older choir members. Make it known that these honors come with being a sixth grader. The sixth graders will feel privileged, and the younger children will have something to look forward to.

3. **Prepare them for youth choir.** Whet your sixth graders' appetites for the youth choir experience that awaits them next year.

Consider separating sixth graders into their own small group during the latter part of the choir year. Let them study some youth choir music and highlight the different voice parts in preparation for this new kind of music reading. Talk matter-of-factly about the male voice change and what the boys can expect vocally in the future.

Comments from a Child Therapist

Remember the demands, fears, and anxieties of middle school and early adolescence? Someone described adolescence as learning three foreign languages simultaneously: the language of emotions, the language of physical hormones and changes, and the language of peers. The pressure and stress of growing up may be highest for sixth to eighth graders.

Boredom, psychologically, sometimes means that a child is not sufficiently challenged or utilized. Sixth graders often feel trapped between childhood and adolescence. If they are grouped with younger children, they may feel insulted. If your sixth graders quickly master their parts and otherwise seem bored, get them to be small-group leaders.

Sixth graders need constructive ways to burn off tremendous physical, emotional, and social energy. To younger children, sixth graders seem almost grown. Sixth graders make excellent junior teachers and can help younger choir members by giving them important one-on-one attention and coaching. If you have a small group of sixth graders that has no interest in leading younger children, see if they can form a trio or quartet which would be challenging and give them a unique identity.

Concluding Encouragements

Comments from a Choir Leader

Who needs discipline? Both children *and* their leaders need it.

What kind of discipline do they need? The answer to that question is not quite as simple.

At times, children (and adults) need just a little positive reinforcement to get them through some hard work, a temporary crisis, or a case of the wiggles. Some directors can hold a rehearsal together with entertainment tactics or by the sheer force of their personality, but our goal should extend far beyond these coping mechanisms. We must strive to inspire in ourselves and in children that deeper discipline which comes from within: *self-discipline*.

It is indeed a fortunate choir leader who on Sunday morning observes a member of his or her choir singing congregational hymns with correct posture and joyful energy. Or perhaps your choir can savor a rare moment of accomplishment when the children realize they have sung a song beautifully for the sheer joy of it. In both cases, if only for an instant, self-discipline is shining through.

Such evidence will never be seen in many of the children we teach. But we are called to continue *planting seeds* and to trust that, in God's time, they will take root and grow.

This brings us to an important point about how you treat yourself. Someone in your choir may exhibit a behavior problem that is too severe or complex for you to solve. You may try every method, trick, and principle in your repertoire and still be unable to cope successfully.

Hear and believe these words: *it is not your fault*. It is wrong and self-defeating to always presume that a child's behavior disorder is a reflection of your teaching.

Love and accept the child as well as yourself. If necessary, enlist another adult or two to help you endure the behavior.

Yes, we all need discipline, but discipline alone is only the beginning. We also need the added ingredients of confidence and faith— confidence in our ability to offer authentic music ministry to children, and faith that God's spirit will complete a good work in us and in the children whose lives we touch.

Comments from a Child Therapist

As you work with children, remember that they perceive life and the world in a radically different way from adults. Keep this difference in mind so you can build trust, respect, and love in your choir.

While staying on task and working from a plan with specific goals are important things to do in choir, it is also essential that children be allowed to share their stories or their understandings of a song, or to put some experience to music that describes what they feel, see, touch, and understand.

Music has the power to simplify and strengthen our faith in God, in ourselves, and in each other. Shared songs blend human experience and emotion into one voice and heart. The music from deep inside us takes our life experiences and our understandings into account while we sing from a common and familiar script.

Certain songs take on their own meaning, in part, from the memories of childhood. At reunions and diverse gatherings of people, hymns and spirituals call people back to their faith, their feelings, their values, and a closer relationship to God and Jesus.

By the age of five, children can understand concepts of love, grace, forgiveness, hope, and resurrection because their hearts and minds are united. Ironically, it takes years of learning and living to get back to the natural instincts and clarity of childhood.

Music affects us all—children and adults alike—in so many ways.

Notes and words enter our senses and give us energy, courage, joy, and pleasure. Whether we worship in large sanctuaries or small chapels, through music we can hear the faith, hope, and love mentioned in 1 Corinthians 13 swirl above us and fall gently into our hearts and minds. We can feel accepted, loved, and united, and in harmony with the people and places of this impressively complicated and wonderful world.